Leveraging Up!

Brilliant Points of Wisdom for
Administrative Professionals

JOANNE LINDEN

CPS, CEAP, CWCA
Educationist & Author

Published by Joanne Linden and AdminUniverse™

Printed in the United States of America by Author2Market.

ISBN: 978-1-7348954-1-4

DEDICATION

At the writing of this book, the COVID-19 crisis has taken an unimaginable human toll and financially has ruined billions of businesses globally. So many are suffering and often overlooked are the charities and non-profits. I am choosing to donate any profits from this book to a charitable organization. In honor of my father who suffered from this debilitating disease, proceeds from this book are being donated to benefit Alzheimer's and dementia care, support and research programs. It is my hope to see this disease eradicated during my lifetime, so families do not have to witness their loved ones slipping away before their eyes.

For more information on the charitable donation visit me at https://AdminUniverse.com/LeveragingUp

ABOUT THE AUTHOR

Joanne Linden is an educationist, author and consultant. She is the master trainer for Star Achievement Series® Certification & Designation Course at AdminUniverse™ and the Founder & Chairperson of the Administrative Center of Excellence™ (ACE-EA). Linden is a Certified Professional Secretary, Certified Executive Administrative Professional, and Certified World Class Assistant. She completed a Leadership & Communications Course from UC Berkeley Haas School of Business in conjunction with OfficeNinjas leadership program. With more than 30 years as a Silicon Valley Administrative Assistant, Joanne previously held the title of Chief Executive Assistant at Synopsys for over 19 years.

A true activist for professional administrators, Joanne, along with other CEO assistants, developed the first certificate program for Administrative Professionals with UCSC Extension in Silicon Valley. Joanne served on the Advisory Board and has been an instructor for that program. Linden served both as a past member and Chairperson of Silicon Valley Catalysts Association (SVCA) and past President of the International Association of Administrative Professionals (IAAP), San Jose and Crossroads

Chapters. Joanne currently serves as a board member and was the Chairperson for the Silicon Valley Admin Awards Advisory Board's inaugural year.

Joanne along with Linda McFarland, co-authored the book *Sitting on a File Cabinet, Naked, With a Gun: True Stories of Silicon Valley CEO Assistants.*

TABLE OF CONTENTS

INTRODUCTION

Executive and Administrative Assistants must perform a unique balancing act in the professional world, juggling their time and attention between keeping their Managers on track and managing an Administrative team under them. As the President and Master Trainer at AdminUniverse™, I've noticed some common struggles most assistants face as they enter the work force. There's the struggle to meet the needs of demanding Managers; the struggle to find their own leadership style; the struggle to set up and maintain a positive office environment—all while finding some space in between to unplug and replenish themselves so they don't burn out.

If you find yourself facing one or more of these challenges as a Professional Assistant—or if you're simply feeling overwhelmed at the prospect of starting your first job—this book is designed for you. In the following pages, I've curated some of the most poignant articles from the AdminUniverse blog and boiled them down into usable **"Points of Wisdom"—practical bits of knowledge that you can easily absorb and integrate.** These Points of Wisdom are hard-earned from my many years in the Administrative space, and they

continue to serve me today. My hope is that by sharing them, emerging professionals like you can effectively skip some of the "hard knocks" I've taken as you find your own path toward success.

To make the information easier to navigate, I've broken the book down into four parts. The first section, "Developing Synergy with Your Manager," will be especially helpful for Assistants just getting started, or for those who work with Managers who are particularly demanding. The second, "Developing Effective Leadership Skills," is designed to help Assistants who are responsible for managing a team. The third part offers tips and principles for developing a positive and diverse work environment. We close with "Being and Doing Your Best," which offers practical tips for building your own professional skills while taking personal time to unplug and regroup.

At the end of each part of the book, you'll find a section called "Action Steps" with some practical questions for applying what you've just learned and reinforcing it in your memory. I recommend you don't skip over these sections, but instead take a few minutes to reflect on what you've learned and imagine how you'll apply it to your life. By doing so, you'll begin to see how these Points of Wisdom can truly change your career for the better.

Since this book has been curated from our blog, you may notice some repeating ideas popping up in multiple areas. I purposely left it this way because those ideas are worth reiterating multiple times in different ways for the purpose of positive reinforcement. I want these ideas to become second nature to you and repeating them will help you remember them when needed.

As you implement these truths in your personal and professional life, I'm confident they will make your work easier and propel you to higher levels of success as an Administrator. I wish you the very best on your journey. Here's to your success!

As we start the age of cocooning our workers at home, over communicating with your teammates is a good thing.

-Joanne Linden

PART ONE

SYNERGY WITH YOUR MANAGER

Making Remote Communications Work

Aligning Expectations

"My Manager Doesn't Like Me"

Admin Partnership Styles that Work

Getting Your Manager to Say YES

Managing a Brilliant C-Suite

Action Steps

The one who follows the crowd

will usually get no further than the

crowd. The one who walks alone,

is likely to find himself in places

no one has ever been.

-Albert Einstein

MAKING REMOTE COMMUNICATION WORK

As an Administrative Professional, you're tasked with providing the necessary support to help your Executive conduct company business on a daily basis. But in today's world, it's not always possible or feasible for the two of you to be in the same room together. Suppose your Executive is sent on an extended trip overseas; suppose one or both of you is homebound by illness. Or perhaps a road closure from a mudslide, wildfire or snowstorm prevents one of you from making it to the office. What can you do to maintain instant communication when time-sensitive decisions must be made, or important documents must be signed?

Here's the good news: Thanks to modern technology, we now have many tools at our disposal that no longer limit company business to the office. With a bit of planning and minimal setup, you can put contingency plans in place to use these tools to interface with your Executive from pretty much anywhere in the world. Let's explore some of the ways you can prepare to conduct business remotely, even for extended periods of time.

Setting Up to Telecommute

On days when it's not feasible for you or your Executive to be in the office physically for any reason, setting up a secondary workspace at home or via your laptop is easier than you think. One of the most secure ways for Execs and/or Assistants to work remotely is through the use of cloud-based computing, particularly a configuration that allows for "virtual desktops"—a system that allows you to log into your workspace from any computer. This kind of setup not only allows you to stay up to speed on your current task list from anywhere—it's also secure because all sensitive information is stored in the cloud and not on anyone's personal computer. Talk to your IT department about the best ways to set up your Executive, yourself and other relevant members of your team with remote desktop access.

Remote Communications Tools

In theory, you should always be able to reach your Executive via phone from anywhere in the world—but sometimes you need more than just a phone call or text to conduct business.

For example, you may need to host a meeting with several members of your team, or you may need to coordinate a video conference with your Executive and other C-suite members from various remote locations. Let's look at some online tools you can use to keep these communication lines open from anywhere using either a computer or mobile device. (Not a comprehensive list.)

- **Zoom**—This app is rapidly becoming one of the most popular video conferencing apps because it is so easy to use. People can join you in a video conference simply by clicking a link. Talk one-on-one or in groups.

- **Slack**—A great platform for teams and collaborations, integrating chat, file sharing and phone/video chat in one location.

- **Cisco WebEx**—Another excellent video collaboration tool designed around a virtual "whiteboard" where call participants can contribute ideas in real-time. (Think of it as a conference room with a whiteboard, except online.)

- **FaceTime**—If you and your boss both use Apple devices, FaceTime is a fast and easy way to video chat quickly one-on-one.

- **WhatsApp**—A great lightweight tool for communicating internationally via text, phone or video chat.

Getting Important Signatures Remotely

If you need your Executive to sign important paperwork but you can't get in the same room together, many e-signature apps now make it easy to scan documents and have your Executive sign them electronically from anywhere with an Internet connection. DocuSign, PandaDoc, and HelloSign are among the most popular of these apps, and they all offer similar benefits.

Other Tips for Conducting Business Remotely

While these tools all make remote office communications easier, they can also make your workflow more cumbersome if you don't use them wisely. Some additional tips to simplify the process for you:

- *Set up your apps before you actually need them.* Waiting until you are in a remote situation before considering remote applications can cost you valuable time (not to mention annoy your boss).

- *Digitize as much of your paperwork as possible.* Many offices nowadays are already going "paperless," so this task should be relatively simple.

- ***Establish set "check-in" times with your Executive.*** If you're working in different time zones, this tip can be particularly useful in keeping communication lines open rather than interrupting your boss at inopportune moments—or vice versa.

Keeping communication lines open remotely may not be as convenient as working together in the office, but with the right technology and a bit of pre-planning, you can make the process nearly seamless. Be sure to consult with your office IT department to ensure you understand your online tools and how to use them to your best advantage.

I'm often asked by Executives

"Find me a mind-reader."

Like in any relationship, the ability

to mind read comes with time.

-Joanne Linden

ALIGNING EXPECTATIONS

It's the first day of your new job or your new role. You prepare the perfect outfit; you place each hair in perfect order. Perhaps you take some extra time to apply your makeup flawlessly. You step into each shoe with purpose. Quickly you tap the buttons, and the coffee begins to percolate. You breathe in the aroma and think forward to your day—how you will carry yourself, making certain to smile at everyone, settling into your desk and approaching each task with determination.

Just as you envision your day and how to best set yourself up for success, you should begin having some "vision-casting" conversations with your Manager from day one. Prepare your own list of personal expectations that you must meet in order to fulfill your own personal goals, along with another list of how you want to meet specific goals within the company and some plan to get there. When you sit down with your Manager, have these ready to communicate, as well as asking what the expectations are for you in your role.

Why Is This Important?

Demonstrating how proactive you are willing to be, not just about their expectations for you, but about meeting your own personal goals and goals that you yourself see as productive for moving the business forward, this will communicate your dedication for your role immediately. This is the best first impression you can give for your new Manager, this will be the first seed to grow their confidence in you.

Must You Discuss the Goals from Each Side?

Believe it or not, your goals may be different. They may all be designed to contribute to the bigger picture and overall success of the business, but you must keep in mind that your Manager has a point of view that is unique and seasoned. Your Manager has had the experience to see the reality of the bigger picture, and ultimately your Manager will be the one who determines what goals you are responsible for. This doesn't mean that expressing your own goals is moot – in fact, it speaks volumes about your ability to look forward to the future and plan accordingly. Anticipation for any situation means you can prepare yourself to the best of your ability. Who wouldn't want to see that quality in their new employee, or someone in a new role under them?

Special Note to Executives

Just as your Assistant is preparing to meet your expectations as well as planning towards their own personal growth, you should be making sure to initiate those conversations about expectations early on. The confidence to step up and start these conversations with a new Manager doesn't always appear right off the bat, and that's okay. It's important for you to see Day One as a new page for you both, a chance to clarify the expectations for your Assistant and vice-versa. Nothing plants seeds for a successful working relationship like open and clear communication.

Turn your wounds

into wisdom.

-Oprah Winfrey

"MY MANAGER DOESN'T LIKE ME"

Some relationships just start out rocky. Maybe your Manager misread a facial expression, or perhaps they just had a huge disagreement with their own Manager that morning, and the residue is still on their attitude towards, well... everything. It seems that at certain points in life, we have all had that unfortunate experience of working with or for someone who just doesn't seem to have any bit of desire to accept us, much less like us. However, in the business world, and especially in the workplace as an Administrative Professional, when these situations arise, it is a test of our patience as well as our skill set.

As an Administrative Professional, there is a certain responsibility to find ways to deal with and solve difficult situations. Whether it is a double-booked event, people not showing up to meetings on time, dealing with rude vendors, or just keeping tabs on the office inventory, Assistants are always expected to be on top of it. While this is quite manageable in nearly every other situation, having to convince your Manager that it would be to their advantage to try to like you can be a little overwhelming. Here are 4 Points of Wisdom to identify and deal with those difficult circumstances.

Watch for Warning Signs

Sometimes you won't need any assistance in deciphering this attitude flaw, but even when it isn't apparent, you should always be cognizant when you are in a new role for a new Manager. So, what should you be on the lookout for? How can you tell if trouble is brewing? Here's what you'll notice. If they start to lose trust in you, they'll become very prescriptive in their guidance—they may say, "Make sure you do x, y, and z as you are completing this project." or "Don't book any travel until I approve all the arrangements first."

They'll start checking in sooner and more frequently to see how you are progressing on assignments: "Give me a daily status update on all your projects." If they start to think the misfit is serious, you'll observe them correcting what you say or how you say it. They won't let you finish with your status update before jumping in and telling you you're doing it wrong —a very bad sign.

You will no longer be invited to certain meetings you used to attend. At this point in your employment it's too late. If you get a negative performance review, you are probably close to getting fired. If fortunate, your employer will offer a performance improvement plan. But even if you turn around in 30-90 days, they will still find fault and you may well be gone.

2 Act Quickly

Pay attention to that first time the Manager's guidance feels very prescriptive or more precise than you expected. You're still in what we call the "forgiveness zone," which means you can regain their trust through quick corrective actions. Ask them whether there was something you did recently that triggered their feedback. Have them explain what they would have done differently in that situation. Listen carefully. They are describing their expectations about the right approach to how they want things done or the real priority they want you to focus on.

Adapt your workflow to meet their expectations and make sure to demonstrate, in ways that are highly visible to them, your new behaviors or your heightened emphasis on their priorities. This may seem unwarrantcd to you. But it's important to remember that if you want to succeed in your job, it will always be your responsibility to adapt to your Manager.

3 Discover your Manager's Priorities

So, what's the most likely cause of a perceived misfit? It usually starts with one event. You likely hit one of your Manager's "hot buttons"—their critical performance priorities or style imperatives. For one Manager, maybe you didn't provide timely updates on project status. For another, maybe you met the criteria for the offsite, but they expected you to exceed it. Perhaps you spoke out of turn at a meeting – something they consider a sign of disrespect. Or maybe they wanted a simple one-page itinerary and you provided a five-page itinerary with details they didn't want or need – and they interpreted that as a sign you didn't listen or, worse, that you can't get out of the weeds. Maybe you simply didn't keep them informed of an important set of events that was unfolding, and it took them by surprise.

As soon as you start working with a new Manager, one of your priorities should be to understand their buttons. Ideally, you should ask them directly: What are your absolute priorities for your performance and mine? What criteria should I always consider in decision making? When it comes to style, you should ask: How would you prefer I work with you? What do I need to avoid doing that would really bother you? Find out how they'd prefer to work with you, such as how often you two should meet, whether they prefer formal or informal meetings, if you should always be reachable by email and cell, and how they will measure your performance.

Observe Your Manager's Non-verbal Cues

As an Administrative Professional, you are sometimes asked to be a mind-reader. How to become a mind-reader, of course, is to stop talking, and instead listen and observe. Not every Manager will convey what's important to him or her publicly. So, in addition to asking directly, watch their actions in meetings. Observe what annoys them. Observe what they praise. See which individuals engage them well and ask yourself what it is about them that the Manager finds so engaging. Look at the Manager's style of running meetings and the level of candor and push back between the Manager and the meeting participants. Look at their office – what does it tell you about their lives, their needs for organization, the demands on them, and their preference for scheduling versus spontaneous interactions. If the

Manager had a previous Assistant, ask that person what really irks the Manager – they'll know better than anyone.

Normally, you should wait to solicit feedback on your behavior until you've worked with your Manager for about a month. However, I'd recommend doing so immediately at the end of a meeting where you played a major role. Ask them directly, "What did I do well and what can I improve upon next time?" The most developmentally focused Managers will usually give you concrete guidance about what they want to see from you. Ineffective Managers may not. With them, you'll have to pay far greater attention to their non-verbal behavior for that feedback.

But if you don't ask directly, your Manager usually won't tell you the first time you trigger a hot button. They may assume it was unintentional on your part, but you're now on notice – you just don't know it yet. The second time you trigger them, however, the Manager will begin to doubt you. Certainly, by the third time, you'll hear from them. But at this point, you are now identified as a problem in their minds.

So, in those early days with your Manager, ramp up your observation skills. The first time you trigger one of their hot buttons they'll send you a non-verbal signal. You'll see a raised eyebrow or grimace or hear something like "I personally wouldn't have done it that way." Do not ignore that statement — have a conversation about it afterwards.

One quality that distinguishes individuals with successful careers is an attitude that there isn't a Manager you can't win over – you must understand why they act the way they do. Remember that all Managers want to be successful in some form or fashion. Your mission is to figure out how to help them succeed.

There is no such thing as a self-made man. You'll reach your goals only with the help of others.

-George Shinn

ADMIN PARTNERSHIP STYLES THAT WORK

"Choose a job you love, and you will never have to work a day in your life." These words are attributed to Confucius, the famed Chinese Philosopher who died in 479 BC, and since then the quote has been pointed toward more modern-day alumni; nevertheless, the adage still rings true today. But simply "doing what you love to do" may not be enough when you are part of a corporate environment.

Whether it's working directly for the CEO or as an Administrative team member, you will find the "work style" of your Executive or Manager will have an impact on how you perform and enjoy your job. How many people do you know who have quit a job because of their Executive, supervisor or team leader? I am guessing at least a few, or perhaps you left a job because you didn't fit the mold your Executive required. I've heard the stories. He was too demanding. She was a micro-manager. I never received any direction or support, or (the other extreme) I work better when left alone. Whatever the reason, disappointment in many cases can be cut off at the pass by finding a partnership style that works with your Manager at the outset. Here are a few Points of Wisdom to consider:

Observe and Make Mental Notes

Gain perspective on your Manager's preference for on-the-job behavior by watching how he or she interacts with others, conveys expectations, evaluates efforts and results, and makes decisions. How does your Manager prefer to communicate? During meetings or one-on-ones? Is he or she in control of every aspect of decision making or open to delegating tasks and responsibility? Over the course of several days or a few weeks, you should have a grasp of your Manager's work style. In the rare circumstance you find you are perfectly aligned with work ethics and work style, enjoy! Otherwise, there's some work to be done.

Evaluate your workstyle, then list any behaviors that may be out-of-sync with your Manager's expectations. Or if you're interviewing for a job, during your interview process ask questions such as "Do you prefer to communicate in one-on-one meetings or via email, texts, etc.? Do you delegate tasks and responsibility, or do you prefer to maintain control of all aspects of your job?" Also, ask what their management style is with their direct reports. This will give you a good picture of how they would work with an Assistant.

Adapt and Evolve

Whether it's brainstorming with co-workers, submitting your ideas in writing or tackling several tasks at once, approach new ways of doing things as a learning experience that could help you improve your skills. It may be challenging, but you just might find yourself stretching yourself beyond what you thought were your limits. And that is not a bad thing. If you are struggling to adapt, but are committed to success, there are "third party" or "Executive" coaches you may consult to help you hone the skills needed to achieve your goals.

Stay Classy

If your Manager or their management style becomes the topic of conversation with co-workers, strongly resist the urge to join in the banter. Whether legitimate or not, discussions regarding any Manager or supervisor with other employees could result in dire consequences. And besides, you are better than

Leveraging Up!

that. Any issues (no matter the employee) should be discussed directly with the Manager, a superior or Human Resources if warranted, depending on how the chain of command is set up in your workplace.

Notes

Don't panic, rather look for alternatives to just "getting a raise" with "I'm a valuable asset and here is why."

-Joanne Linden

GETTING YOUR MANAGER TO SAY YES

From "quality of life" requests like a stand-up desk or ergonomically correct chair; to office upgrades such as new software or equipment; and of course, the daunting task of requesting a raise, promotion, or attending training or professional conference; getting your Manager to say YES is all about how you make your case. Here are 5 Points of Wisdom that can help:

Plan, Plan and Plan Again

Define your request, your reasons and why it would be advantageous for the Manager to say yes. Anticipate objections and obstacles, then weigh the odds of actual success. If it looks like your request is reasonable, make plans to go for it, but make sure your timing is right. If the company is in the middle of downsizing, cost-cutting, or your Manager is struggling with a "full plate," you might want to wait until circumstances improve.

If A then B – Mom's Quid Pro Quo

As a child, I remember refusing to eat certain vegetables (okay I admit it...any vegetable), until my mother said, "Joanne, eat your broccoli, and you'll get dessert." She was inadvertently schooling me in the "art of negotiation" with her "if A then B" technique. If you have an important request, such as a promotion, by all means, let your Manager know why you believe you deserve the job, but also point out how the company stands to benefit by employing "If A then B." By example "If I can take on this additional responsibility for supervising the team, they will field their questions to me, leaving you more time to focus on those sales goals." Or B, "This promotion benefits both of us; by allowing me to have more responsibility in the office, I'll gain more experience while you work on growing the company."

Short-term View Achieves Long-Term Goals

For example, if the option to work remotely occasionally doesn't seem to be something your Manager will embrace, you may want to propose a trial run. After all, a "try out" could be much easier to get approved and could lead to a permanent change if it works out for all involved.

4 When the Answer is Definitely No!

Accept it, but also know it's reasonable to ask what it would take to change the answer to yes. If you're turned down for a raise because there is no money in the budget, ask if your request would be considered during the next round of budget planning. If you're turned down for on-the-job reasons, ask what you need to accomplish in order to earn a raise in the future.

5 When the 30-Second Elevator Pitch Becomes Handy

With its name derived from the time it typically takes to ride an elevator with a "captive audience," this short spiel is usually intended to introduce yourself to a potential employer or customer. It can, however, be used for minor requests such as "we need a new coffee maker." "Hey Boss, I've seen a lot of stale coffee being poured down the drain, so I did some research and found a new 'one cup per serving' machine will end the waste and eventually pay for itself in the savings realized from more efficient use." Have support materials should you need them, but keep

Leveraging Up!

your pitch clear, concise, logical and include benefits to your company and/or Executive.

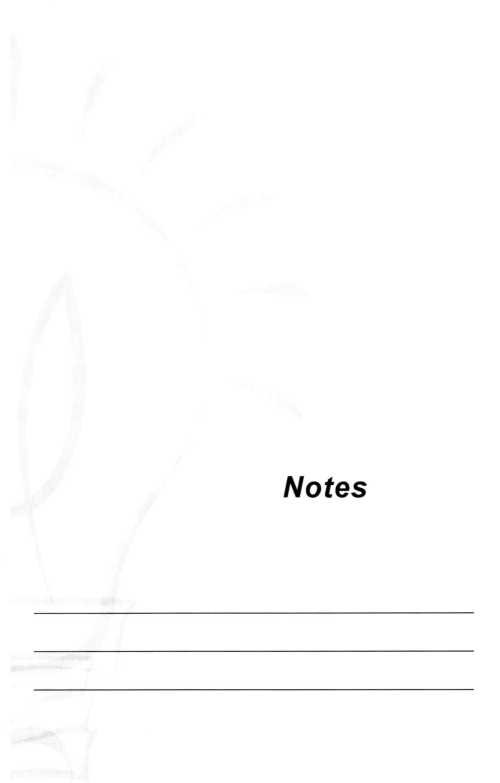

Notes

_____

_____

_____

Another day goes by

and I'm thankful for my

rewarding career as an Admin.

-Joanne Linden

MANAGING A BRILLIANT C-SUITE

Assistants juggle a lot of responsibilities and are constantly organizing the flow around the office and what should be funneled to their Executive. Think about all the ways we plan for our Executives, from their daily agendas, to the outlines for their meetings, when they will speak to whom – even what office supplies to use. A mark of a phenomenal EA is how well they manage their Executive. It should really leave everyone wondering, "Who is the Executive?"

It's not a case of being abrupt, demanding or confrontational, but more about using the skills that you have acquired throughout your career to coax them into assisting you in fulfilling the demands of your role, and in turn fully supporting and assisting them. To help EAs and Administrative Assistants evaluate their performance and opportunities, we have created 5 Leadership

Skills to leave them guessing about who's managing the Manager. Here are some Points of Wisdom to consider:

Schedule Time

It's no secret that your Executive is incredibly busy and finding time to break away from their daily routine/schedule for even five minutes to have a catch up could be incomprehensible to them, or they may think it's not necessary.

Think about what time you need with them and how frequently. It may be that you'd like to sync up with them each morning for five or ten minutes to discuss the day's agenda, and then have a 30-minute meeting every other week to discuss any other business or forthcoming appointments. Look at their calendar and see where you can schedule in the time to meet with them – it may be five minutes before the working day starts, or five minutes at the end to iron out the "ins" and "outs" of tomorrow.

Schedule in your slot and send your Executive an invitation – with a message which states why you have selected this slot and what you would like to discuss – e.g. "I would like to sync up with you first thing tomorrow morning to go through the following points…"

or "You have a meeting with Mr. Jones tomorrow at 10am, the notes for the meeting are attached – need to run through a few points beforehand at 9:50am." You'll find they will be hard pressed to decline the invitation if you clearly confirm the reason for the meeting and outline your agenda, making it clear as to why the meeting needs to happen. To ensure the meeting is not overlooked once it is agreed to, make sure you "flag it" – this will highlight that the meeting/sync up is important, and ensure it doesn't "slip" their mind.

Regular meetings with your Executive are crucial for the development of your working relationship, as well as getting to know and respect each other on a more personal level – any Assistant and Executive who have a great relationship will tell you this.

Put Yourself in Their Shoes

In order to be able to work with your Executive and support them to the best of your abilities, you need to understand how they operate, what their role entails, and get into their frame of mind – put yourself in their shoes. What areas of the business do they operate within? Are you well versed in these areas?

If not, it may be time to look at expanding your role and the support you offer by getting to grips with the real intricacies of the role of your Executive. If they are in the field of finance, embark on a short course or seminar which will enable you to gain an insight into the areas in which they operate. This will undoubtedly help your career no end; having knowledge and skills in a different sector of industry, but also being able to support your Executive while being more attuned to their role.

A management or leadership course could also be a great way to get into the frame of mind of your Manager and allow you to understand and grasp their role more intimately. This will not only give you more confidence and the opportunity to expand your expertise and, in turn, your career progression, but it will also enable you to gain a deeper insight into the demands, pressures and requirements of your Executive's role, and enable you to support and manage them more efficiently, on a genuine level.

Look and "Be" the Part

You might have heard the adage, "Dress for Success," and though the saying is correct in the first impressions, it is just the tip of the iceberg in the concept of "Look and Be the Part." The way you look and present yourself in your role is not solely about the way you dress – although it does play its part. Being the best EA you can be in order to support and manage your Executive is about always remaining professional, presenting yourself in the best possible light and seeking out ways in which you can continue progressing in your career and assisting your Executive in progressing in theirs.

Look for ways in which you can stand out and really take command of your role. This could be anything from making a conscious decision and acting outside your comfort zone; to requesting training in new areas of the business; to requesting funding/investment to attend an industry event or seminar which will enable you to network with your peers and learn tips on how to progress in your role; to putting yourself forward for a new project. If your Executive sees you are serious and passionate about your career, they will understand how important it is for you to succeed in assisting them and should not really want to hinder your career progress.

Your Executive/Manager needs to have the confidence that you are fully capable in your quest to support them and know that you are serious about having a successful career. Once the penny drops, and the results start showing up, they will subconsciously be more open to your managing them. Your goal is to aim high, step out of your comfort zone and find achievement in supporting them by becoming their strategic partner and ultimately culminating in their success.

As with professionals in any area of industry, there may be people within the company who the Executive does not necessarily get along or "gel" with. As an EA, this is simply not an option. It's up to you to cultivate a favorable working relationship in which you both are working together in harmony, and in effect making each other's lives easier. This may not necessarily be on the top of the list of important things to do for your Executive, but it has to be on yours, in order for you to be as successful as you possibly can be.

A good relationship between the two of you is the foundation from which your career can succeed and progress. If you refrain from tackling any issues you have which prohibits you from carrying out your role effectively, be assured your personal and professional growth will be stunted, as will the progression and perception of the profession overall.

Communicate on The Same Level

Communicating effectively with your Executive may come naturally to some, especially those of us who have invested many years growing into our roles. However, many EAs find themselves shaky and unsure when they are speaking with their Executive.

Your Executive can smell fear. When you are communicating to your Executive, you need to be on their level. You need to understand that what you are communicating to them is important to their performance and overall, the success of the company. The value you see in your role will determine how you approach your Executive.

Learn how to navigate the communication with your Executive in a way that is direct—logical but respectful. Learn to speak with presence, whether it is for a room full of Executives or just your own Manager. Between the two of you and your roles, no one has time for misunderstandings or overly emotional responses. If something is wrong, address it directly in a timely manner and prepare what will happen next as a solution to move forward. This is generally where most EAs get tripped up. No one likes delivering unpleasant information, but to move forward, this element of communication is crucial. Master learning how to deal with difficult situations with tact and facts and be able to speak to your Executive about any subject, on their level – they will respect you for it.

(5) Mutual Respect

Throughout the journey of developing a strategic partnership with your Executive, they will be evaluating your performance, your attitude, and skills. The way you handle yourself will determine how the level of respect and mutual trust will grow. Seeing your authentic desire to dedicate yourself to your role as a leader, as well as an Assistant, will only encourage them to respect you more.

It doesn't stop there. Assistants must learn to have respect for their Executives. It is true that some are a little easier to respect than others, but there is always somewhere to start. Perhaps you have respect for their visions, how far they have come, what they have accomplished, how they achieved success. Start there. Respect grows with focus on the positive. The amazing thing is that respect begets respect. If your Executive sees that you have an honest respect for them, theirs for you will grow.

Notes

_____

_____

_____

ACTION STEPS

As you take a moment to reflect on some of the key points of the past few chapters, ask yourself the following questions. Feel free to write down your answers:

1. If you have somehow gotten off on the wrong foot with your Executive, what steps can you take now to win them over?

2. Think about something you'd like to ask your Executive for (e.g., a promotion, raise, attend a conference, etc.). How can you phrase the request in an "If A then B" format?

3. Thinking about the chapter on "Managing a Brilliant C-Suite," what are some things you've done right? What are some areas you could improve on? What steps will you take shore up the weak spots in your professional style

Notes

Highly successful organizations and individuals all have an extremely clear vision of where they are going.

-Lawrence J. Peter

PART TWO

DEVELOPING EFFECTIVE
LEADERSHIP SKILLS

Leadership Skills You Need to Develop

Office Leader or Bully?

How to Become a Subject Matter Expert

5 Ways to Fix the Kinks in Your Team Alignment

Action Steps

Clarity of Mission. Excellence in Execution. Approaching every task with this focus on accomplishment guarantees successful engagement.

-Allan Linden

LEADERSHIP SKILLS YOU NEED TO DEVELOP

For most Administrative Professionals, leadership skills do not flawlessly develop overnight. They are collected and refined over time. Let's explore 7 leadership skills needed to improve both resume development and role effectiveness.

Communication

Communicating as a leader is a magical craft. As an Administrative Professional, you communicate with a multitude of personalities on a day-to-day basis, so it is necessary to master the art of personalized communication. Be mindful that everyone has a different style, that circumstances may dictate reactions, and that your own emotions can misrepresent or betray you if you are not consciously directing all types of communication.

Leveraging Up!

As a leader you must fight not to gossip, be judgmental, show negativity, have too many excuses, lying and dogmatism. Communication starts with honesty. Be authentic, be yourself, show integrity, become your word, and be empathetic by wishing your listener well.

Forms of Communication

It's interesting to note that *Verbal Communication* is present in both spoken and written words. Both forms require the use of professional and tactful choices of words, but the spoken form has an emphasis on tone, emotion and quick-thinking. Remember, words can be compared to a tube of toothpaste. Once you squeeze the paste out, you can't put it back.

Non-Verbal Communication takes the form of smiling, laughing, waving, gesturing, pausing, and so on. Many people are not aware of how often they communicate non-verbally, and therefore they do not take the opportunity to curate their "silent words."

Motivation - As an Administrative Professional, you may find one or more of your team or co-workers portray an attitude of being unproductive, lazy or absent-minded. Developing a plan to help motivate may just be the key factor to rehabilitate and release their potential.

Administrative Leaders have access to a view of the office and/or organization that no one else has. Step back and take a 10,000-foot view of the personalities and relationships in your team and determine how they perform and interact. This is a valuable tool you may not even realize that you have at your very fingertips.

Forms of Motivation

Praise – A close friend shared a story of when her daughter was playing on a soccer team that just could not win a game. She saw the disappointment and lack of enthusiasm take their toll on her little girl and the team. As a leader at work, my friend used her talent of giving praise to each of the players by standing on the opposite side of the field calling out the player's name when they were near. Praise is an incredible attitude and morale booster. She said the positive effect of calling out names combined with appreciative words of the teammate immediately motivated them to play harder, and eventually the team won a few games.

Leveraging Up!

When you think about it, often when employees begin to underperform, you can track the behavior to a feeling that they are not appreciated or inadequate. If that is the problem, expressing appreciation and encouragement is a great way to solve their lack of motivation.

Setting Smaller Goals is a solution for when you have identified that an employee is feeling overwhelmed or that expectations may be a bit lofty. By working with them to develop manageable goals, it not only communicates that you are aware and care, but it also helps them to mentally accomplish a goal in bite-sized pieces.

Incentives are always a fun and creative way to motivate your team – especially if you do it on a budget. You don't have to spend a lot of money to make a big impact. A small budget is sometimes better as it forces you to release your creativity, making the event more enjoyable for you and fun for the team. Creating contests with fun prizes will spice up the work week and give the employees something to re-focus on.

Positivity - As an Administrative Professional, you are the beacon that guides your office into a positive mental space. Many will confide in you, ask for your advice, and come to you for comfort – so it is important to equip yourself with a positive attitude and methods to lead your team in creating a welcoming and happy atmosphere that will allow everyone to thrive.

Tools for Developing Positivity

Conflict Management is a great way to foster positivity between colleagues that may have trouble getting along. Conflict arises in every office, and many times it's up to the Administrative Professional to detect conflict and either mediate personally or alert the Human Resources Department. Conflict Management techniques will help to eliminate negative occurrences and act as preventative measures for the future.

Empathy is an important skill to practice for when people are having a difficult time. Throughout the week, different team members may be struggling with various personal issues that could affect their performance at work. Being able to identify those circumstances early on and deal with them in an empathetic manner will strengthen relationships in the office and provide comfort to those who are dealing with rough situations.

Keep in mind that people deal with situations differently. What you consider to be inconsequential may be life-changing for someone else, so don't assume they are overreacting.

Encouragement is one of the biggest components for a positive environment. Most often when work is suffering, it is due to a lack of appreciation for the work they are doing. Even small recognitions for a job well done will serve to encourage people and uplift their spirits and positivity. Take the time to send a quick email to a colleague recognizing the success of a recent offsite or pulling together a last minute all hands meeting. Take it a step further and copy their Manager.

Humor is a wonderful relief from the day-to-day stress that accompanies any office. When used appropriately, humor can bring so much light and positivity into the environment and changing attitudes from negative to positive!

For example, my CEO had a favorite mug that he took to all his meetings, but he had a habit of leaving it behind in conference rooms. Ultimately the mug would resurface, but during a particularly stressful time when the mug went missing, I looked high and low and could not locate it. I decided to have some fun and lighten the mood in the office. I cut out different size letters from magazines and crafted a ransom note that read "Send $5 to POB XYZ or the mug gets it." I delivered the note during our daily 1-on-1. With a very serious tone, I said I had received this very disturbing message and handed the note to him. We had quite a laugh over it. Just remember that you need to know when the time is right to use humor and how it will be received.

Creativity - As a leader, you will often be faced with problems that require a little more thought, or an out-of-the-box solution. Creativity is a great way to set an example of unique problem-solving techniques.

Tools for Building Creativity

Conceptualization requires experimenting with ideas in an abstract manner, strategizing outwardly whether verbally with a group, or on paper. Many times, it is only after forming and re-forming ideas over and over, that you finally curate the final and most efficient version.

Identifying Patterns can be used to observe human behavior and identify trends. In the office this can translate into finding what incentives continually motivate productive behavior, or inversely what types of situations are occurring within the office to provoke negative responses. Once you pinpoint winning combinations, you are well on your way to building a stronger and more efficient team, while pro-actively avoiding obstacles that prevent your team from reaching their full potential.

Open-Mindedness is key to exploring new options. Instead of focusing on one result, examine the surrounding factors. Taking time to step back and observe the big picture in context and being open to hearing all sides of a story will help you to reach an approach to understanding how things truly work and how to improve them.

Feedback

As a leader, you should always be seeking to acquire feedback from your team to evaluate the effectiveness and progress of any process – especially when it is a new process that has been put in place. Additionally, this is a great way to open conversations about the performance of individuals in your team. Constant evaluation is key to building a stronger workflow in your office.

Tips for Developing a Good Feedback System

Be Approachable. If your team doesn't see you as approachable, it will hinder the amount of feedback and the authenticity of what type of feedback you receive – whether it is about a process, their performance or even your own. Always ask and listen first. If someone even senses that they are being attacked by the way a question is asked of them, or if a conversation begins with an accusation, your team member is likely to shut down or only focus on defending themselves. Make sure they feel that speaking with you is a safe space and that their opinion is respected.

Clarify Expectations. Clarity is key. Be candid – straightforward and honest about what you expect of their performance or of a specific process. Make goals clear, concise and achievable. When it comes to individual expectations, this should be catered to the team member's abilities. Since no two people are the same, individual expectations should be tailored in a way that will not intimidate them to the point that they give up. You want to provide an opportunity for them to feel motivation through confidence allowing them to flourish.

Leveraging Up!

Follow Up with your team after any feedback is received. You want them to feel that their opinion is valued, and they need to be aware that you are taking things seriously in evaluating any circumstance. This is especially important when dealing with conflict. Following up shows that you care about their well-being as well as the morale of the office.

Notes

If your actions inspire others

to dream more, learn more,

do more and become more,

you are a leader.

-John Quincy Adams

OFFICE LEADER OR BULLY?

You've heard the phrase, "no one likes a bully" and for the most part, "everyone loves a hero." A bully wants to gain power and control people, a hero wants to empower people and help them thrive. Which would you rather be?

As an Executive Assistant to a CEO or other high-ranking staff member, you have the opportunity to assume a leadership role in the company's Administrative Community and accept the unwritten job requirement to be a company champion for Administrative Professionals throughout the organization. As you assume this role and go about managing workflow and/or effecting change to Administrative systems, here are some Points of Wisdom for becoming the office hero, not the office bully.

Take a Look Around and Ask for Input

Soak in the atmosphere of the workplace and ask others what they like, what they don't and what could be improved. Really listen to what they say, then decide what is working well, what ideas or changes are worth pursuing and which ones are unlikely to happen. Get started with the small stuff to show you are committed to your team. Tweaks like flavored coffee, a faster printer, employee of the month or birthday recognitions, set you up as an "office hero" who is interested in the comfort and productivity of the team. For larger issues which require more planning to solve and often more money, set up a priority list for your Manager, along with the "input" received from staff members. Your initiative will likely result in some positive changes and impress your Manager too! Nice perk!

Stay Calm and Assert Yourself!

We've all had those days when nothing seems to go right, or something dreadful occurs. When a missed deadline, a disgruntled client or office drama warrants a confident approach; take hold of the situation with clear thoughts, an even tone, and matter-of-fact demeanor. It is much easier to accept (even from people who don't agree with you) than an aggressive approach featuring hot tempered orders and pronouncements. One too many outbursts and you could be labeled an "office bully." On a side note, even though "swearing" seems more commonplace these days, foul language should not be used in an office setting (that goes for acronyms too). It can offend and detract from your professional position. For example, a former Manager of mine had been promoted to the Vice President of Sales. From my desk outside his office, I would listen to his conference calls with his sales team and cringe each time he dropped the "F" bomb. After one such call, I summoned the courage to confront him. I explained that as the VP, he needed to set a professional example, that he wasn't "one of the guys" anymore and that he needed to curb his language. He thanked me profusely as he wasn't even aware he was doing this.

It's All About Attitude — Be An Optimist!

Studies have shown people who "look on the bright side" are more likely to get help when needed and are generally more "well-liked" than pessimistic types who rely on "woe is me" and negative comments throughout the day. As an Executive Assistant, a positive attitude definitely comes in handy when juggling many tasks or asking for assistance. As an added incentive, optimists tend to live healthier and longer lives. Be

Leveraging Up!

happy, be healthy and be an "office hero." If you have trouble embracing the "sunny side" seek advice or professional assistance to help turn your viewpoint around.

Notes

_____

_____

_____

The key to becoming a Subject Matter Expert is to educate yourself on something that motivates you. Then share that information.

-Joanne Linden

HOW TO BECOME A SUBJECT MATTER EXPERT

Think about how you add value to your role. How is it that you go above and beyond your duties as an Administrative Professional to keep your Executive informed? We all know the chaos that can ensue during certain parts of the year. Your Executive has so much to juggle – the very reason our role exists in the first place – so being able to keep up on the trends and become a Subject Matter Expert is a phenomenal way to evolve into higher positions.

The key to becoming a Subject Matter Expert is to educate yourself. The following insights will help you get started incorporating self-education into your routine.

① Become an Insatiable Reader

"Insatiable" is the perfect word for the attitude you need to have to become a Subject Matter Expert, or just to keep up with trends. It means that you have a true desire to consume, which in this case would mean to consume information. How do you do this? Grab those magazines at the store, anything business related, and start to catch up on them during breaks, before or after work. This is also a great reason to utilize that "Bookmark" function on your browser. Create folders for the top business publications, podcasts and social media. Make it a point to dedicate at least 30 minutes to exploring and reading these resources each day. You can also sign up for the emails – but do this with caution and create filters to keep them from overwhelming your inbox.

② Be Smart About Social Media

Most of us have that weakness for browsing mindlessly through Facebook or Instagram, just curious as to how others are living life and what memes are the most popular of the day. Did you know that there is a way to utilize Social Media that will end up being an asset to your career? For this we recommend having dedicated "Education" accounts. For example, if you are browsing Instagram, don't do it from a personal account where you will be tempted to wander onto friends' profiles and other novelty reading. Creating an account specific to the information you are trying to learn will create a barrier from anything unnecessary. On this account, you will only follow relevant business accounts and hashtags. It's a great way to keep up with trends, especially on one of the most popular social media accounts for both personal and business. If there are important customers or competitors you want to watch, set up a Google Alert for those companies or executives and be the first to alert your Executive on important announcements.

Follow Money Trends

Pay attention to where your companies invest their money—including at your own organization. This includes keeping an eye on venture capital, private equity, and the public markets, as well as where clients (mostly IT and marketing departments) are spending their dollars and what kinds of people they are hiring. Money flows toward ideas that people think will succeed. A pattern of investments in particular areas will give you clues to what might be the big ideas over the next five to ten years. Depending on the industry you are working in, you will be able to tailor these searches and have a wealth of information to present to your Executive.

If everyone is moving

forward together, then success

takes care of itself.

-Henry Ford

5 WAYS TO FIX THE KINKS IN YOUR TEAM ALIGNMENT

Just like having your spine aligned to allow for proper circulation and energy flow, aligning with your team creates a work environment that is not only efficient, but incredibly productive. To some it may mean that everyone is getting on the same page with the details, where others may see it as taking a look at the bigger picture. Regardless of why they feel alignment is important, proper team alignment is essential to helping your teammates to stay focused and maximize profits for your company.

With the growing amount of competition, businesses can't waste time ignoring this important success factor of aligning their team. Here are 5 Points of Wisdom that are essential ways to align focus and get your team back on track:

Don't Rely On He-Said-She-Said

Remember that game we used to play as children? Telephone? A line of people forms, and the first person begins by whispering a phrase into the ear of the person next to them. By the time this whispered message traveled down the line, it was hilariously unrecognizable when compared to the real thing. Communication can happen just like that in the office; however, it doesn't always end in laughs, but rather conflict. Skip the game and make sure any information you are receiving is coming straight from the source.

Relate Routine Efforts to Overall Goals

This will enable Managers and employees to more clearly visualize how their team and individual work contribute to the larger company strategies and success. Sometimes people lose track of how even the smallest routine task is benefiting the end-goal. Everything matters, so creating an environment of performing with intention is crucial to drive a business to success.

3 Every Team Member Must Commit

It's about accountability and moral support. If everyone is participating together to accomplish a goal, there will be conversation about it, shared struggles and triumphs, and an overall sense of team accomplishment once the goal is met. What better way to get everyone aligned, than to help them visualize and commit to this train you are all aboard?

4 Recognize, Reward and Play to Strengths

It is no secret that positive feedback will work as a type of incentive to motivate your team members to keep going strong. A Gallup study found strengths-based employee feedback resulted in a 12.5 percent increase in productivity.[1] Understanding what employees' strengths are and utilizing them to align employees with the company's goals will help everyone succeed, so pull out a notebook and start observing.

---

[1] Aniruddh Haralalka and Chee Tung, Leong, "Why Strengths Matter in Training," Business Journal, April 3, 2012.
https://news.gallup.com/businessjournal/153341/why-strengths-matter-training.aspx.

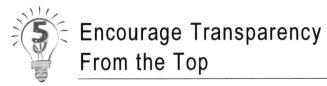

Encourage Transparency
From the Top

Creating an environment of honesty and openness contributes to the positive morale in the workplace. It is important to maintain a high level of transparency throughout the entire company and allow leaders to see the productivity of employees – to ensure that all team members are working towards the same goals.

When properly implemented, team alignment can be the defining factor in the success of a company. Adjust your focus to align team members and get them on track by staying committed to the company goals, being transparent and communicating directly to the source. This will help your team feel more engaged and motivated to play a role in the company's success and stay aligned with its goals.

ACTION STEPS

As you take a moment to reflect on some of the key points of the past few chapters, ask yourself the following questions. Feel free to write down your answers:

1. Review the 7 leadership skills we discussed. Which of these skills do you feel you have in spades? Which skills do you feel need some improvement? What can you do to shore up these skills?

2. Think about becoming a Subject Matter Expert. What type of subject matter would be most useful for your career? What can you do to educate yourself and become indispensable to your company on that topic?

3. If you manage a team, what are some ways you can identify that your team is out of alignment? What can you do to fix those kinks?

Notes

_____

_____

_____

When in doubt, check if

your actions are aligned

with your purpose.

-Azim Jamal and Brian Tracy

PART THREE

NURTURING A POSITIVE OFFICE CULTURE

5 Amazing Benefits of Cultural
Diversity in the Workplace

Making the Workplace Inclusive for
People with Disabilities

Show Intolerance the Way Out

Weaving a Workplace Tapestry

Action Steps

Create caring and robust connections between every employee and their work, customers, leaders, Managers, and the organization to achieve results that matter to everyone in this sentence.

—David Zinger

5 AMAZING BENEFITS OF CULTURAL DIVERSITY IN THE WORKPLACE

From an Administrative Professional's perspective, it is hard to visualize culture change, especially in a position with limited authority – yet every voice matters. Cultural diversity in the workplace is when companies are open to hiring employees from all sorts of different backgrounds regardless of race, religion, culture and educational institutions. When companies recruit and retain a diverse pool of people, it brings about various benefits to the company as well as its employees.

Though there are numerous benefits, diversity in the workplace doesn't come without its challenges. As the Administrative Professional, you have a unique vantage point to communicate and unite the team members and foster collaboration in the workplace.

Improved Productivity

A diverse company can lead its employees to greater productivity. Diversity brings different talents together, all of them working towards a common goal using different sets of skills.

Companies will also gain from each employee by learning from each other's experiences and applying this new-found knowledge to their work. Employees from all sorts of different backgrounds get to learn from their colleagues' experiences from a different perspective. Thus, they are able to bring fresh ideas to the project by thinking outside of their comfort zone.

Increase in Creativity

Another benefit of cultural diversity in the workplace is the increase in creativity among teams, and the ability to have a more diverse set of solutions to specific problems. It's a dream team of Assistants that can bring a global perspective in solving challenges and improving workflows.

With so many different and diverse minds coming and working together, many more solutions will arise as every individual brings in their personal way of thinking, operating and solving problems and making decisions. Companies that encourage diversity in the workplace inspire all their employees to perform to their highest ability.

 ## Improved Team Engagement

A proven way to learn about other cultures and ethnicities from colleagues is to hold an internal networking event, asking fellow Assistants and co-workers to join in during a lunch break or after work. Ask Human Resources or Head of Diversity to speak on key results expected by having a pool of diverse employees and how each other's lifestyle and culture sets the course and direction for the organization.

When the team members share personal experiences about when they were in high school or what different holidays or seasons mean to them, they build a trusting relationship among their colleagues. Team building through understanding each other's diversity is a great way to build morale.

4 Reduced Turnover

A company that embraces cultural diversity in the workplace would immediately entice a wider pool of candidates for its job vacancies. When companies recruit from a diverse set of potential employees, they are more likely to hire the best of the best for the industry.

In an increasingly competitive economy where skills and talents are crucial to improving the company, putting together the most diverse set of candidates is necessary to succeed in the market.

5 Improves Insights and Reduces Racism

A dream for some Administrative Professionals and reality for those enjoying a more culturally diverse workforce, it is often found that employees then spend more time in their daily lives with people from cultural backgrounds that they are often never exposed to. The result is that employees learn new cultural insights and this in turn, reduces negative emotions such as racism, homophobia, sexism and the like.

Notes

_____

_____

_____

Excellent firms don't

believe in excellence –

only in constant improvement

and constant change.

–Tom Peters

MAKING THE WORKPLACE INCLUSIVE FOR PEOPLE WITH DISABILITIES

With all the conversations arising about embracing diversity and working towards a welcoming and inclusive environment in the workplace, the discussion about people with disabilities on the workforce has yet to receive as much attention as its counterparts.

Despite this information proving that those with disabilities create the largest minority group in the country, many companies are still ignorant about learning who these people are and how to create a work environment that fosters inclusion and productivity. In an effort to help Executives and fellow Administrative Professionals to guide their workplace into a better position of hiring and retaining people with disabilities, here are 5 Points of Wisdom that you can take:

Make a Bold Statement From the Top

As an Administrative Professional, you have the opportunity to bend the ear of your Executive and share not only any observations you have noticed within the workplace environment, but additionally you can offer solutions to foster a welcoming and accepting and functional atmosphere.

You can note that guidance toward an inclusive business culture starts with senior leadership making a commitment to hire people with disabilities. This transparency from the leaders of the business will send the message through the whole structure of the company that people with disabilities are valued, and that the company will support those who face trauma or disability throughout their career to be successful.

Educate Yourself

Remember that people with disabilities are not a homogenous community. In addition to spanning every race, nationality and ethnicity, people with disabilities may have blindness or be hard of hearing; have chronic conditions like lupus or multiple sclerosis; have intellectual disabilities or autism spectrum disorder; or have psychiatric disabilities like depression, anxiety or bipolar disorder. (Consider that many disabilities are invisible to observers.)

Take the opportunity to educate yourself on the many types of disabilities that are common in the workforce, and how to best accommodate those individual situations. Sharing this knowledge with your team will help guide their communication and collaborative efforts when a person with a disability is brought on-board to join the team.

Create a Workplace Culture Where Requests are Heard

Be aware that it is not always easy for people to request something specific that would help them to get their job done more efficiently, especially since you may have workers with invisible disabilities who don't feel safe disclosing them. Whether it is a desk, technical aids, or some other piece of equipment, team members should feel comfortable enough to address their needs.

Leveraging Up!

As an Administrative Professional, your role in this is not only to spread the knowledge and awareness, but to keep a watchful eye to notice when someone may need something extra to aid in their productivity – in the event that they are not comfortable enough to ask for it.

4 Recognize Those With Disabilities Who Deserve It

Incentives and recognition events are a wonderful way to boost morale across the company. Those who have gone the extra mile to contribute to the success of the team should be praised, and this is a fantastic event for the Assistant to organize. In the planning stages, make sure to take into account those with disabilities who have been going above and beyond as well.

5 Learn the Right Terms

Many individuals prefer people-first language that emphasizes the person instead of the disability, i.e., "people with disabilities." And though the use of the label "differently abled" has gained some traction in recent years, it has been dismissed as euphemistic. Just ask someone what term they prefer instead of assuming. It's just being respectful of people's language choice.

Ultimately, it is important for all the team members in any company to be aware of the diverse physical and emotional needs of their array of employees. Making people feel accepted and supported is the key to strong positive morale within your workplace. Be the leader that sets the tone and opens the discussions to educate and spread knowledge throughout your office!

To improve is to change; to be

perfect is to change often.

-Winston Churchill

SHOW INTOLERANCE THE WAY OUT

Any organization's ability to thrive depends greatly on people being willing and able to work well together. How well your team members share ideas, engage in robust debates and make decisions influences the extent to which full potential is realized. How people learn and move forward together is fundamental to your organization's ability to survive and thrive.

As an Administrative Professional, you have the opportunity to mold the attitude towards diversity in your office. Here are 3 Points of Wisdom that Administrative Professionals can utilize to influence sensitivity and tolerance in the workplace:

Lead by Example

Never lose sight of the effect that your attitude has on your workplace environment. Reflect on the ways in which you influence tolerance. Do you bring an open- and fair-minded approach to your role? Do you influence the way leaders in your organization view diversity and the power of difference? Do you demonstrate patience when dealing with emotional issues?

As the Administrative Professional, you are a central link in the company. Your ability to communicate with everyone in the workplace makes you the best venue to share your knowledge and lead by example.

Educate

Take steps to educate people about the link between respectful conduct and the ability to leverage a diverse team through collaboration. Begin by helping people appreciate the power of diversity and teach them why tolerance and sensitivity matter to building great relationships with anyone, but especially those who are different to them.

Help people understand that, frequently, with differences come challenges. An inability for people to appreciate and work constructively with those who are different to them is a common roadblock to team success. A lack of understanding often leads to a lack of tolerance and in turn insensitivity.

Set Clear Expectations

Define what it means in your workplace to behave with respect and sensitivity. Work with both your Executives and the members of your team to clearly articulate what successful behaviors look like, as well as those considered damaging and undesirable. Take the time to ensure every member of your team understands what is expected, and that Managers know how to reinforce expectations.

How do we create a harmonious society out of so many kinds of people? The key is tolerance — the one value that is indispensable in creating community.

-Barbara Jordan

WEAVING A
WORKPLACE TAPESTRY

As Administrative Professionals, we are required to be leaders in communication and interpersonal savvy throughout the workplace. Interacting with a multitude of different personalities, communication styles, backgrounds and cultures is to be expected, so naturally we must set an example to help others communicate and work well with those around them. First, we must make certain that we have sharpened our skills to best connect and communicate with our team. Cultural Competence is arguably one of the most valuable skills for efficient workplace performance. But what does it mean to have cultural diversity in the workplace? Culture refers to the values, norms, and traditions that affect the way a member of a group typically perceives, thinks, interacts, behaves, and makes judgments. It even affects perceptions of time, which can impact day-to-day scheduling and deadlines.

Leveraging Up!

Simply put, "cultural competence" is the ability to interact effectively with people from different cultures. This requires individuals to be aware of one's own cultural world-view, knowledge of other cultural practices and world-views, tolerant attitudes towards cultural differences, and cross-cultural skills.

As a growing amount of different cultures are working together, the more cultural competency training is essential to avoid any problems that could arise in the workplace. Cultural problems can range from miscommunication to actual conflict, all endangering effective worker productivity and performance. Below are 6 Points of Wisdom to help your team embrace and welcome cultural diversity in the workplace.

Communication

As mentioned, Administrative Professionals must be proficient in communication, as we become the pathway in which crucial information is carried throughout the workplace. Providing information accurately and promptly is critical to effective team performance. This is particularly important when a project is troubled and needs immediate corrective actions. Being aware of any language barriers that may exist is the first aspect in paying attention when delivering or receiving instructions. It is important to comprehend how instructions are communicated through verbal and non-verbal language that deliver positive or negative reactions. Good communications start and end with clarity and to ensure a positive outcome, remember to get clarification on any areas that need further explanation.

Team Building

Fostering an atmosphere where everyone can work together in an effective and productive manner is part of being an Assistant. We are the beacon it seems, the point-of-contact among so many moving parts (and people). So initiating and leading activities that will help exercise those team muscles is crucial to building trust, understanding and collaborative skill in the workplace. These team-building activities will encourage communication and cooperation from one team-member to another – making it necessary for each person to learn how to communicate with the other to achieve a common goal.

Schedules

Navigating the daily timetable is something we are very familiar with in the Assistant world – not just for ourselves, but for so many around us. Having the awareness of the different cultural and religious events happening will help us to anticipate when members of our team will be absent to observe those events. This anticipation is an incredibly important way to circumnavigate any potential hold up that employee absence will create which may hinder the progress of an active project or even the daily flow of work. This will allow time to use our problem-solving skills to find a solution that will cater to both the employee and the rest of the workplace.

Attitude and Awareness

We all know about a little thing called, "attitude"! We deal with it daily, which is to be expected when connecting with as many people as Assistants do. Attitude is about an individual's perception of something, and their reaction to it. We must be aware of both of those components. Understanding why an individual has a certain perception requires knowing a little about their background and culture, as does understanding their reaction. For example, some cultures are raised to keep their emotions suppressed, which may result in a miscommunication if you were raised to be more expressive. It is important not to make snap judgments about the way you perceive someone to be reacting – you must examine why. Sometimes, this is as simple as asking clarifying questions. The bottom line is to understand that communication is a little different for everyone and giving them the chance to be understood makes a world of difference. We can lead that wave of learning to understand.

5 Knowledge

We've all heard that saying, "the more you know". As Assistants, continuous learning and education is important to us – it motivates us and drives us to reach goals and help others. We have many opportunities to educate those around us – this is where you can get creative. When it comes to learning about different cultures, reading does a world of good. Make time to examine publications from around the world, as well as podcasts or blogs about cultures. These days, the resources for learning are vast. Maybe you've noticed that there is a large portion of your office that is bilingual. Create activities and opportunities to learn those other languages. Maybe a language a month and encourage others to learn through activities. Embracing cultural aspects that are dear to those team members around you will not only make them feel included but valued.

6 Skills

The goal of training – in awareness, attitude, and knowledge – should be skills that allow organizational leaders and employees to make cultural competence a seamless part of the workplace. The new work environment is defined by understanding, communicating, cooperating, and providing leadership across cultures. Managing cultural diversity in the workplace is also the challenge for organizations that want to profit from a competitive advantage in the 21st century economy. Whatever ways you decide to educate your workplace about valuing the cultural differences around you, those efforts will help to promote an accepting and welcoming atmosphere in your office. In turn, you will notice how this change in attitude will create forward motion, leading others to communicate efficiently and work together towards success!

Notes

_____

_____

_____

ACTION STEPS

As you take a moment to reflect on some of the key points of the past few chapters, ask yourself the following questions. Feel free to write down your answers:

1. Do you consider your workplace a diverse workplace? If not, what actionable steps will you take to encourage more diversity? How will you lead by example to "show intolerance the door?"

2. Office diversity is about more than race, religion, gender, sexual orientation or being differently abled. It's really about learning to embrace our cultural differences and how different people see the world. What will you do to help your office become more culturally competent? What can you do to open your own world-view wider?

Notes

_____

_____

_____

Great things in business are never done by one person. They're done by a team of people.

-Steve Jobs

PART FOUR

BEING AND DOING YOUR BEST

6 Ways to Enhance Your Creativity

6 Tips for Maximizing Your Productivity

Peer Learning: When Admins Learn from Each Other

Your Time is Precious

Conquering Workplace Challenges by Focusing on You

Action Steps

We all have expectations. Aim high and stretch yourself, you'll be pleasantly surprised at what you can accomplish.

—Joanne Linden

6 WAYS TO ENHANCE YOUR CREATIVITY

Administrative Professionals are planners, organizers, strategists, and key collaborators with their Managers and peers. Many Assistants will be the first to claim they aren't creative, but what they don't realize is that much of their work process relies on creativity. To hone your creative mind, and give a high-level view of the integration of creativity into your daily workflow, we've compiled a list of 6 essential tips for developing your creativity at work:

One-size Does Not Fit All

While a quick Google search can point you to a list of articles flaunting 100 tips to improve your creativity, it's important you remember, what works for them may not work for you. For instance, while music may enhance your friend's creativity, for you, it may serve as a mere distraction. Instead, map out a creative process fitting your task or goals. Paired with your job and abilities, you'll be surprised at how often you're already using creativity to solve daily work challenges.

Think Visually

Regardless of your role or responsibilities, researching data and ideas is an incredibly effective way to see your creative vision. Some office challenges might prompt you to stop looking at the screen, get off your chair, and make your way to the whiteboard. Even consider bringing your team or peers along with you for inspiration—all the while promoting collaboration and leadership.

Get Physical

Engaging in physical activity can unlock your mind and bring clarity to thinking. Simple mental breaks will promote greater overall health and better focus on your tasks. Take a walk outside or consider going for a jog. Jogging at work is no easy task, but it sure clears the mind.

4 Take a Break

The worst killers of creativity are dreaded mental blocks and burning out, both tough things to avoid. It's essentially impossible to nurture creativity when you're suffering from one or both. Sometimes, we all need to take a step back and allow our tired brains the ability to reboot. Once the mental break has served its purpose, let the creative juices return to normal schedule.

5 Treat Yourself

Rome wasn't built in a day. Reward your successes, no matter how small. Without them, the long-term goals will never be met. A word of caution watch your calorie count and put your credit card away. There's a thin line between the proper amount of treat vs addictive behavior when using "I need to treat myself."

6 The Creative Process

The foundation of creativity is learning. As you hone your creative thinking, you'll go on to invent new processes and produce innovative ideas. In essence, you'll flourish. Remember, nothing is off the table or too outlandish. Buts and ifs have no place in the realm of creativity.

While creativity isn't a one-size-fits-all ability, it is the root of individual success. Though some industries permit a more evident stance than others, it is undeniably the essence of any efficient company.

Notes

_____

_____

_____

The true sign of intelligence

is not knowledge

but imagination.

—Albert Einstein

6 TIPS FOR MAXIMIZING YOUR PRODUCTIVITY

As an Administrative Professional, managing your day is the most important way to set yourself up for success. Obviously, this is a highly valuable concept to implement for your Executive as well, being that they depend on their Executive Assistants for the structure in their days. Being able to learn these 6 productivity tips and being able to pass them along to your Executive will strengthen your partnership, add value to your role, and launch you into further success! Check out these Points of Wisdom:

Give Yourself a Break Every 90 Minutes

Our bodies operate on an energy cycle of 90-minute intervals throughout the day. When we've been working on something for an hour and a half or longer, it's natural that our alertness levels will go down and our attention will wander, or we'll feel drowsy (or start checking LinkedIn, Twitter, Instagram or Facebook).

The counterintuitive secret to sustainable great performance is to live like a sprinter. In practice, that means working at your highest intensity in the mornings, for no more than 90 minutes at a time, and then taking a break.

So, the next time that drowsiness begins to take over, step away from your work for a few minutes instead of pouring another cup of coffee. You might be surprised how much you'll get done in the long run.

Create "Do Not Disturb" Signals

How frustrating is it when you are just getting into the zone on a big project and then one of your colleagues decides to visit your desk? Worse, research shows it can take up to 25 minutes to get back on track after an interruption.

Whether you need to stay focused on intense tasks for a couple of hours a day or you're working on a big project, using a system that informs people of this will get them into the habit of sending you an email for non-urgent tasks instead of dropping by your desk.

A new method of signaling that you should not be disturbed in the office is to put a "Cone of Silence" onto your desk to communicate to the team that you need to be able to focus at that point in time, and you should not be disturbed unless there is a dire emergency.

3 Energy management

You know it's important to budget your time wisely— but it can actually be more effective to also manage your energy. Optimize your workday by doing your most concentration-intensive tasks during peak hours, when your energy levels are at their highest.

If you're a morning person, do your most important tasks first thing and save the tedious, mindless tasks for later in the day when your energy is waning. Not sure what your peak hours are? Try energy mapping to find out and make the most of your workday.

4 Don't Be a Slave to Email

Try checking email only at specific times of the day. Easy to say, but as an Assistant, hard to do. Why? Instead of feeling that you have to respond to emails the minute they hit your inbox, you can save time and stay focused by setting a schedule for checking and responding to email. Checking email only twice a day is not practical for Assistants, however, checking once an hour is still effective. Shut down Outlook, turn off new email notifications on your phone, and do whatever you have to do to muffle the interruption of email.

Depending on your position, this may not feel like an option— especially if your Manager or colleagues rely on you for quick responses. But you may be surprised at how supportive people will be about your new productivity strategy when you explain it to them. You can also set up an auto-responder with a message explaining when you'll be checking email again and how people can get in touch with you if it's important in the meantime.

5 Keep your Emails Short and Sweet

Executives don't have time for reading novel-length emails—or writing them, either. Challenge yourself to think critically and efficiently when connecting via email or any other form of communication.

By keeping emails short and to the point, you'll not only save a lot of writing time, you'll also save your co-workers a lot of reading time. If your issue is too complex for a short email, scheduling a brief (5-10 minute) phone call can be much more efficient than a lengthy back-and-forth email exchange.

Delegation is Your Friend

It's easy to get overwhelmed by feeling that you must do everything yourself. Delegating, however, is one of the best ways to manage your time. Passing projects off to other members of the team lightens your load and lets you focus on the projects that you do best.

Delegating doesn't mean trying to get out of doing your work—but if you have too much on your plate, delegating one of your tasks to another member of your team can help devote more attention to your more pressing projects. Don't have a co-worker who can take on your task? You can try outsourcing your dreaded tasks to a freelancer on Fiverr.com.

Leveraging Up!

Taking control of all the various tasks on your to-do list may sometimes seem impossible, but if you try making these small changes, you'll be amazed at how much you can accomplish during your workday!

Notes

_____

_____

_____

Recipes tell you nothing.

Learning techniques is the key.

–Tom Colicchio

PEER LEARNING: WHEN ADMINS LEARN FROM EACH OTHER

Peer learning has become extremely popular in academic settings, but how does it work among the office? Well, pretty much the same way. Creating an environment where Administrative Professional team members are comfortable to ask each other for help and in turn, help each other, is going to completely evolve your workplace in terms of morale and productivity. How can you do this? This works best when you have teams collaborating on the same project, or have a common goal in mind, but once it is part of your office culture, you will see it manifest in even daily tasks. Here are 6 Points of Wisdom that are essential to incorporate into your peer learning:

Leverage Common Threads Among Participants

Peer learning works best when participants have a lot in common in their roles, functions or issues. What is important to everyone involved? Is there something at stake, a shared challenge, opportunity or goal? Multi-organization peer learning groups are likely to have shared focus areas, like a joint project or a community population they serve. For peer communities within an organization, focus on needs or challenges that span departments or center on organizational strategies.

As you identify the common thread that drives the need to connect and learn from one another, consider aligning groups around:

- Position or title.

- Level in the organization.

- Experience level.

- Function, duties, and/or responsibilities.

- Specific challenges, industry pressures or initiatives.

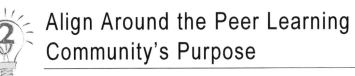

Align Around the Peer Learning Community's Purpose

Stakeholders — sponsors, program staff, community partners, champions and participants — all have goals and expectations about what participation in a peer learning program will yield. Discover an intersection where a goal can fulfill multiple stakeholder objectives. Verify the value of the purpose with the different groups involved. Based on the needs, you can innovate and experiment with the best facilitation methods, frequency of interaction, online tools, success metrics and length to achieve those objectives.

However, a major pitfall occurs when the organizers or sponsors of the peer learning community are unaware of or disconnected from the participants' current context. For instance, a sponsor might want the facilitator to say, "Tell us how you're implementing your quality improvement plans," when in reality, few people in the group have the resources to even get started on a quality plan.

Peer learning facilitators help bridge this gap by returning to the common purpose, starting with the current reality, then growing capacity to move toward the desired future.

Focus on What Matters Most

Check in with participants individually or in small groups to find out what is top of mind or keeping them up at night. To create a core of engaged, enthusiastic colleagues who help keep discussions dynamic, check in with members by email or phone; ask specific individuals to share their ideas or experiences in an upcoming discussion, or invite members to present or be a case study.

Prepare for your conversation to be as concise and engaging as possible, especially when speaking to busy staff whose participation might be limited by their availability to work outside their normal scope of work. Consider an informal advisory committee of active participants to identify their top issues, goals, challenges, opportunities, topics of interest, etc. Participants often appreciate being asked for their guidance. What's going on in their world? What value could the peer learning group offer them? Share topics you are considering and ask participants to suggest specific angles or examples they'd like to explore.

4 Build Trust and Camaraderie

Peer learning facilitators, listen for themes, capture key ideas and resources, maximize time, and create opportunities for participants to bond. Participants can concentrate on sharing and learning, knowing that one person is keeping the conversation on track and moving forward.

Ensure everyone feels safe and has a chance to participate. Psychological safety is an important component in willingness to learn, the sharing of ideas and admitting mistakes. Set aside time for participants to get to know one another before tackling heavy topics. Acknowledge and normalize the discomfort of being vulnerable and set confidentiality guidelines. During each new peer learning community's first session, ask everyone to agree to the terms of confidentiality, thoughtful discourse and respect toward one another.

Next, be aware of status dynamics — participants might be unwilling to share their challenges if the assistant to their Manager's Manager is in the same peer group, or if an unfamiliar person is in the room. Fireside Chats are now a popular session in which participants have an informal, engaging and in-depth question-and-answer session.

5 Difference is a Point of Value

Diverse perspectives can help us transform our thinking. When participants' perspectives differ, normalize their experience by sharing how groups often come from different perspectives, but can still work together on a common goal. We often ask participants to consider how they can apply parts of another's experience to their own work, and how that perspective might also be true. Participant check-ins will help you understand and prepare for differing perspectives.

6 Make Data-Driven Improvements

Regularly collect quantitative and qualitative data from participants about their experience. Develop processes to capture data such as attendance trends, peer learning participant turnover, participant satisfaction with meeting facilities, and progress on team goals or objectives. Useful qualitative data includes participant feedback about what they valued, how the peer learning information has or will change how they do their jobs, and their ideas for upcoming sessions. This data will not only help program staff learn how and where to improve, it will demonstrate program value to stakeholders and participants.

By considering these points when designing and implementing a peer learning community, a program can flourish as participants collaborate and stakeholders realize their goals.

BONUS: 3 Ideas to Start Peer Learning Within Your Admin Community

No matter how big your company is, you can start a peer learning program without much investment. One of the strengths of this type of learning is that it can be done rather informally. Here are three things you can do to kickstart peer learning at your company:

Learning Lunches

Many companies have instituted a learn-at-lunch program, and you can organize one in just a few minutes. A learning lunch is simple: everyone in a group, department, or company gets together on a certain day to have lunch together (you can have the lunch catered or just ask everyone to bring their lunch). During the lunch, one person presents on a topic of interest.

The restrictions you place on the topic are up to you; some companies encourage their employees to talk about work-related things, and others leave it completely up to the presenter. Either way, people are learning.

You can also choose the frequency that works best for your group; you might do it weekly, monthly, or quarterly (though more often is probably better). The level of formality is also up to you. If you think your employees would be willing to put together a short presentation, feel free to ask them to! If you think they'd rather keep it as informal as possible, that's an option, too.

Mentoring

Mentoring is a great example of peer-to-peer learning, even if it doesn't feel like traditional training. It's not always focused on an issue or area, but mentors are great at helping newer employees solve problems they're facing.

There's a very strong social component to mentoring, and that's one of its greatest strengths, which is why it's important that mentors and protégés have a good social relationship. Not everyone is cut out to be a mentor. But those who are can be a huge credit to your organization. Is your Manager or Executive a mentor? Who do you look up to in your Administrative team or network and could they be a mentor?

In addition to sharing knowledge, effective mentoring builds strong relationships within your organization—the importance of which can't be overstated. Both parties gain a great deal in the process, and your company benefits in the long run. With structure, a bit of training, and the right format, a mentoring program can help your employees learn more relevant, practical information than they could ever hope to with traditional training.

3 Employee-accessible LMS

Learning management systems (LMS) often focus on top-down knowledge sharing. But that doesn't have to be the case. In fact, we argue that it shouldn't be the case. Learning platforms are perfect for distributing knowledge between employees throughout your company.

Leveraging Up!

Flexible platforms make it easy to share a variety of content. It could be presentations for people to read over, documents that employees find useful, webinars, or just a simple list of tips that someone has learned throughout their career.

If employees are going to use the platform in this manner, though, they must feel comfortable doing it. Employees need to be given agency over what happens on the training platform. That's what drives engagement with learning. You can extend this beyond your learning system as well—a company communication tool (like Slack or HipChat) can become a fantastic learning tool if you encourage employees to use it as one.

The simple act of making it easy for employees to share knowledge might be all you need to foster a learning atmosphere in your company.

Notes

_____

_____

_____

Lack of direction, not lack of time, is the problem. We all have twenty-four hour days.

-Zig Ziglar

YOUR TIME IS PRECIOUS

We live in this intense world. A world that teaches us not only to multitask, but to do it with a sense of urgency. Although being able to juggle different tasks and do it quickly and efficiently is fantastic for your role in the office, it may not be so great if you don't set boundaries for yourself. Taking time to relax and have fun is not something that is spoken about as often in the business world, but it just as necessary for being a productive power player! Here is our quick and easy method for making sure you are a Rockstar at work and at home.

Prepare

You may have heard me say this before – preparation is the key to success. Getting all your ducks in a row. Especially if you are that particularly gifted type of person who constantly gleans inspiration from everything in your environment – take the effort to really reach outside your responsibilities. If that sounds familiar, I'm looking right at you today! Your personality is the most prone to working endlessly, ever reaching, never feeling like you have done enough. It's a wonderful attitude, no doubt about it, but you are most likely to forget to let yourself rest and revive.

Regardless of what type of personality you have, the most important thing you can do for yourself is to set yourself up for success. Plan ahead. This doesn't need to be an arduous task, and in fact, it doesn't even need to take a long time. Invest 30 minutes to an hour at the beginning of the week to lay out your game plan. List out your tasks, mark those that are high priority. From there, separate them into days — don't put it on yourself to accomplish EVERYTHING in one day. Even if it is possible, spread your tasks out from each other, so your brain doesn't begin nail-biting before you've even walked in the door at 8:00am on Monday.

Once you have everything assigned to different days, look and see if you need to gather materials, print out PDFs, or prepare in any way for each task. You can do this with personal tasks and errands that need to get done as well. After you see everything laid out neatly in front of you, breathe a well-deserved sigh of relief. Take note of how your stress levels will be a little lower throughout the week.

Execute

It's one thing to prepare. Once you have completed that step, you should certainly pat yourself on the back. It is a necessary habit to build into your routine in order to accomplish the next step: execution.

Avoid the temptation to relax after laying out your plan, that you feel your work is done. First thing on Monday morning, you need to make yourself a healthy breakfast, grab your coffee and march into the office like a Rockstar! Take that plan of attack and, well, attack! Get straight to work, going down your task list and take care of each item.

This is the time for you to be strict with yourself, making certain to stay within the timeline you set up. Power through and make sure you complete each task 100%. You can keep track of any obstacles or unrealistic time limits for when you plan out your next week.

Leveraging Up!

Not only will it have an impact on the way your Manager views you and your performance, but you will start to feel a deep sense of confidence and satisfaction with yourself.

Relax

Now allow yourself time to sit back and relax without any interruptions in the form of unfinished responsibilities. After a full week of thoughtful preparation and hard work, you have earned your time off. Keep that in mind throughout your weekend, giving yourself the opportunity to thoroughly rest, do something fun, and indulge a little bit. If you need to shut your computer down, turn off your phone and store them both in another room, then do it! Train yourself to separate work time and "you" time.

If you want to be successful, it is absolutely necessary to invest in yourself. It is not selfish, it is "self-supportive." If you want to be 150% Rockstar, then you must recharge your batteries by setting time to focus on yourself. This could be getting lunch with friends, reading a favorite book in a coffee shop, taking that Yoga class, or just lounging in your favorite pajamas while binging on your latest Netflix obsession.

Sometimes, we get so caught up in the need to work 24/7, that this little ping of guilt hits us the moment we do something leisurely. If that's you, then start to reprogram your mind to understand and embrace those moments you have off-of-the-clock. To be your best self, you must take care of YOU.

Attitude, a powerful word that shapes our world. Stay on top of your world, keep your positive attitude. Others will notice.

—Joanne Linden

CONQUERING WORKPLACE CHALLENGES BY FOCUSING ON YOU

Unfortunately, outside factors can create internal struggles. As an Administrative Professional, I had to resist giving challenges the power to impact my work and/or dampen my enthusiasm. Over the years as an Executive Assistant to a powerful Silicon Valley CEO, I learned from him that preparation is good…but good preparation includes thinking about the "what-ifs" that work-life hands you. Common in many organizations is the question of how to effectively plan to confront the people or things sabotaging your enthusiasm.

Common Workplace Challenges:

Whether you've been at your company two days, two years, or two decades, challenges arise. Some common examples:

- **Unpleasant Work Environment**. It's one thing to dislike your job, but when you feel uncomfortable or physically ill walking into work, the environment may be toxic. Your bad Manager, rude coworker, failure to qualify for a promotion, lack of recognition, or any combination of the four can be to blame.

- **Hierarchy/Bureaucracy**. For years, various groups of people – in the realm of business or politics, have voiced their frustrations with hierarchy. Because of the connotation, it may seem like a bad word. If you're at the bottom of the food chain, it may feel like your voice falls on deaf ears. If you're in the middle of the food chain, well, you're in the middle of everything—higher ups project demands, and subordinates look to you for answers or changes you can't provide. If you're at the top-level, you have the most responsibility—you make the big decisions and give the last word. Everyone looks to you, and that alone is difficult.

- **Difficult Clients or Peers.** As an Executive Assistant, I would sometimes have to deal with demanding clients (both inside and outside of the company). I'm sure you've heard the adage, "the customer is always right." The outdated maxim provides clients or peers a sense of entitlement, impacting your ability to do your job.

Tips for Conquering Workplace Challenges

Whether your light is being dimmed by the environment, process, or customers, you can overcome workplace challenges by focusing on yourself in the following ways:

Boost self-confidence

In the business world, your confidence may gradually deplete as a result of errors made when accomplishing tasks. The difference in levels of confidence comes down to how we react to criticism from those mistakes. Take control of how you feel by implementing these habits:

1. Criticism hurts and letting the criticism roll off your shoulders is easier said than done. Try this: if you hear

something negative, keep an open mind and try to clear the ego. If the criticism is emotional at all levels, try not to let it bother you or destroy how you feel about yourself. Take a breath before you react because good criticism is constructive, listen and learn from it.

2. Increase your knowledge: knowing how to handle issues of all sizes can increase your confidence. Seek out inspiration by attending a workshop or conference, take a course, watch a TED talk, or read a book.

3. Celebrate your successes: self-acknowledgment reminds you that you are meant for the position. It's okay to give yourself a "pat on the back" when no one else does. Famous comedian and author Milton Berle stated: "If opportunity doesn't knock, build a door."

Setting and achieving goals

There's nothing more satisfying than accomplishing a goal or task. With each New Year, one topic that rings out to everyone is that of goal setting. Whether short-term "to-day lists", to longer-term life goals or even those great "bucket-list" items, goal setting works because it provides a platform for success.

Developing your idea, or completing tasks needs a roadmap, and is the start of the goal-setting process. Keep it simple, set the goal, what is the start date and end date? What's your objective?

What's your action plan; how do you intend to get there? To achieve your objective, you'll need an action plan. In doing so, prioritize your tasks and responsibilities before the deadline. Ask for help if needed.

Work/life challenges can render even the best-planned goals useless, especially if you stray away from the plan or strategy. Adapt to change but commit to your vision. You can achieve your goals!

While you can't always control outside factors, you can focus on something equally if not more important, yourself. When you choose to enact positive changes, nothing can get in the way between you and success.

ACTION STEPS

As you take a moment to reflect on some of the key points of the past few chapters, ask yourself the following questions. Feel free to write down your answers:

1. Review the 6 Ways to Enhance Your Creativity. Which of these tips resonated with you most? What specific steps can you take in this area to awaken your creative side?

2. Look again at the 6 Tips for Maximizing Your Productivity. What do you think causes the greatest drain on your own productivity? What will you do to address it based on the 6 tips we shared?

3. What are three things you'll commit to do to practice better self-care?

Notes

Absorb what is useful, reject what is useless, add what is specifically your own.

—Bruce Lee

CONCLUSION

As you've read through this book, I hope you've found at least a few Points of Wisdom that spoke to you on your current journey. Hopefully you've discovered some keys to forming symbiotic relationships both with your teammates and the Executives you serve, as well as ways to create a positive work environment for yourself and others. And hopefully you've also experienced some personal inspiration.

All that said, everyone must find their own rhythm as an Administrative Professional, the same as in almost every other profession. Your path to success will look different than mine did, simply because no two Assistants or Executives are exactly alike. As you develop your career, you're likely to discover some Points of Wisdom for yourself that aren't covered in these pages. (I truly hope so.)

Leveraging Up!

My goal in sharing these truths is not to create any sort of "formula" for success—because there is no such thing. However, as the chapter on "Peer Learning" reminds us, we all have the ability to learn from one another—to compare notes, talk about what worked for us, what didn't work, and what made the work easier. By taking these Points of Wisdom to heart, I believe you'll ultimately come to own these truths for yourself—and in so doing, they will carry you to greater levels of fulfillment and success in your career than you imagined possible.

You've read this far, so you're obviously serious about honing your skills as an Administrative Professional. If this book has spoken to you, I invite you to take some deeper steps with us. AdminUniverse™ offers a number services that include ACE Peer Membership; Elite Admin Training & Mentoring; Recruitment for Executive and C-Suite Administrative Professionals. All our offerings are specially designed to help you take your professional career to the next level. To learn more give us a call at (866) 402-2819 · AdminUniverse.com

I look forward to helping you advance your career!